Beyond the Clouds

Beyond the Clouds

Raju Samal

BLACK EAGLE BOOKS
Dublin, USA | BBSR, India

Black Eagle Books
USA address:
7464 Wisdom Lane
Dublin, OH 43016

India address:
E/312, Trident Galaxy, Kalinga Nagar,
Bhubaneswar-751003, Odisha, India

E-mail: info@blackeaglebooks.org
Website: www.blackeaglebooks.org

First Edition: 1992

First International Edition Published by
Black Eagle Books, 2022

BEYOND THE CLOUDS
by **Raju Samal**

Copyright © Raju Samal

All rights reserved. No part of this publication may be reproduced, stored in a retrieval system, or transmitted, in any form or by any means, electronic, mechanical, photocopying, recording or otherwise without the prior permission of the publisher.

Cover : **Kamala Kanta Rath**
Interior Design: Ezy's Publication

ISBN- 978-1-64560-122-7 (Paperback)
Library of Congress Control Number: 2022951076

Printed in the United States of America

CONTENTS

SAD AND SWEET

In my childhood	9
Your eyes have	10
In my last night dream	11
I held her hand	12
In this my lane	13
The moment	14
So much	15
Let those mad men	16
How is it that the cloud	17
Even your stray	18
When I won a woman	19
It is not that some where	20
To earn a fortune	21
As I come out of the temple	22
Sunday in the park	23
Having spent decades	24
In a confused hurry	25
Art galleries	26
Why do we think so deep	27
Everyday we keep becoming	28
Each moment	29
Briefly our life	30
Everyday at dawn	31
To be born is to get	22
No teacher class room	33
What I have been seeing as many	34
What I really do	35
Why do you weep	36
Now that I am tired	37
To create designer	38
Accumulated wealth	39
Night descends	40

THAT ENDLESS BLUE

Birds in the sky	43
Through that blue sketch	44
At dawn the crow	45
Those great men of power	46
Why do you look at me	47
What difference does it make	48
Stupid man can never	49
Power cut	50
Bored in heaven	51
Sitting on the carpet	52
What is great about	53
One day my journey	54
Come let us see	55
In the palms	56
Be still so that I can see	57
Only when	58
To walk inward	59
When my mind	60
In an evening like this	61
Like the late afternoon sunshine	62

... AND BEYOND

With each old leaf falling	65
Who is going fast	66
When doctors failed	67
What is going to happen	68
Furious flood	69
Since many of you	70
Whatever you think of me	71
Rituals are done	72
Inside the skin	73
When the time to go	74
When the day dawns	75
Time is a river	76
What is that where	77
World has not become greater	78
If I would have loved	79

Sad and sweet

In my childhood
I wished to be young

at youth
I regretted my lost childhood

when middle age came
I regretted
to have lost my youth

today when old

I regret to have
regretted my lifetime

Your eyes have
larger vocabulary
than a lifetime of
love letters

while your words
are slow ripples
on lazy waves

your smile
reveals an entire occean

In my last night dream
I saw
you too had come
to weep at my funeral

the moment I got up
how much I wished
to stay
in that state of dream

keep dying
the rest of my life

I held her hand
in love

she was reluctant

like a tree
refusing
to be green
in spring

In this my lane
people call me mad

it delights me
to let them say so

it is because
they take your name

as the only reason
for my madness

The moment
we begin to analyse
we cease to be in love

what so far
has been our dream

turns out to be
a bundle of decaying materials
blessed with life

the blue look of the sea
is not blue
when each drop of it
is seen through

So much
is missed in life
so much remains unsaid

together as we watch the evening sun
going down the horizon
how differently we are together

let life miss so much
let so much remain unsaid

we are
better what we are

Let those mad men
waste their wealth of time
building palaces in the city

I would spend mine in the wine of love
and share it
with intoxicating version of nature

and then in the grave
when they would complain
of being robbed off everything

I would say
now waste not your precious silence
by turning too much
inside this too little a space

How is it that the clouds
which drop rains
sail away with joy
without waiting for thanks

how is it that
the tender blades of grass
do not complain of pain
when mercilessly
we tread upon them

how is it that
the cuckoo which sings
to bring spring to our heart
does not expect an applause

how is it that
we are so different

Even
your stray glance of love
dear sweet lady
rewrites my life in poetry

when the world's
living process
is hijacked by distraction

how do I expect
your entire love
only to be mine

When I won a woman's love
I thought
I got the most precious

but one thing
more precious than that
I was made to know

that was
when I got
that woman's love lost

It is not
that somewhere
someone is lonely alone

every where
every one is

loneliness
is not that lonely
when we are alone

it is when we are alone
among our own people

To earn a fortune
we go on
removing obstacles from our life

only
to remove obstacles from our life
is what is written in our fortune

As I come out of the temple
spiritually awakened

the cry of beggars
makes me feel compassionate

thus my hand
goes on searching
for the lowest denomination
in my pocket

Sunday in the park

school children
think of homework

parents think of
children's homework

school in the park

Having spent decades
to acquire
my high standard of life-style

desperately I search
for a guide book
to learn
how to start living

In a confused hurry
we run
and keep running
until dusk from dawn

when night comes
in case we recollect
we recollect nothing worth
of the day that is gone

Art galleries
exhibit colors

spilled
from confused minds

visitors admire
and call them modern art

Why do we think so deep
of things
that has nothing to do with
our living at the moment

is it not the way
we mortgage our future
to repair our past

Everyday
we keep becoming
more like a thing

weeping is a luxury
we cannot afford

parting for us
is a sort of routine
and death in the family
a formality

all that we are not ready
to listen
is the wailing of the stranded soul
trapped in our living carcass

Each moment
either events come alive
from the coffin of the past

or my heart
palpitates with anxiety
of things to happen in future

how sad
how much always
I am absent in me

Briefly
our life
keeps separating void from void

briefly it makes us feel
everything here is everything

it is nothing
but a mosquito in our sleep
until a pair of drowsy palms
aim at it correctly

Everyday at dawn
the sun comes
to renew and nurture
all the life on earth

yet nobody looks up
with gratitude
to say thank you sun

when night comes
we do not even remember
whether there was a sun

but the stupid man
runs after name and fame
to be remembered
even after he is gone

To be born
is to get diminished
from boundlessness
to a tiny digit

to have some weight
and get entangled
in the equation of life

until death comes
to hold our hand
and takes us back home

No teacher class room

noisy children
briefly celebrating
overflowing freedom
of their childhood

in the seamless processing
of humans
to become machines

What I have been seeing as many
are indeed
only one in many parts

that is how the world is

the way each one of us
has made it to be

now why blame anyone else
when we have in us a part of everyone
and in everyone a part of us

What I really do
is indeed the opposite
of what I feel I should do

thus I fly heights
with that cage around me
which makes me a captive
in the infinite options
in my wish
that I could have choosen from

Why do you weep
over young man's death

my dear lady

he has only taken
a short route to destination

Now that I am tired
with dull routine of the world
let me celebrate

even
be it sorrow

let my heart be that instrument
of music
which could sing
only when it breaks

and from every broken piece
let me hear the silent tale
of my life that was once a song

To create
designer clothes

big brains
take great pains
to end up in imitating
those men and women
of old stone age

who did not know how
to put on clothes

Accumulated wealth
as keep I kept

with Desire
the alluring mistress
I remained obsessed

most time of life
I knew not how to spend
yet I wanted to borrow
a moment at the time of death

Night descends
in soundless steps
spreading her soothing veil
upon earth's tired limbs

sleepless moon
flirts with floating clouds
audience of stars
twinkle in surprise

the noisy day
like a child
asleep after unceasing cries
rests under shadow of bliss

That endless blue

Birds in the sky
moon in the sky
stars in the sky

most enchanting
of them all
is the stretch of nothingness
in the sky

Through
that blue sketch of infinity

the abstract
is revealed to the human

the way it looks
is not always
the way it is

At dawn

the crow
wakes me up

who wakes up
the crow

Those great men of power
and fame
are now merely some pictures
and words in the pages of history

men of love
with their ordinariness
are the blank space of those pages

once you are there no more
how does it matter
whether you are a written word
or a blank sheet of paper

Why do you
look at me that way

is it love
or it is not

let it be anything
you look at me
that way

says the earth
to the ever-staring sky

What difference does it make

if one dies today
or tomorrow

the day after

it is the same silence
and the same blue sky

Stupid man
can never realise
what it means
to be here on this earth
of beauty and plenty

unless
he comes to know
what is there
elsewhere

and herein after

Power cut

darkness
connecting

man
to the moon

Bored
in heaven

a shooting star jumps

into death

in an attempt
to land
on earthly paradise

Sitting on the carpet
of a white cloud
I took the half-moon
as my cup

and drank that heavenly wine
in the company of learned stars

in that drunken state

I lost my ways of the world
and found
my path to heaven

What is great
about your killing me

in any case
I would have gone there

where you too
will come
when time comes

not to meet me
but to become
part of the same nothing

One day my journey
will end
but this road will not

looking back
I search in vain
for that time-space
when and where
this universe was not

to live
is to live this now
with all that is around

to be able to be
one with the existence

Come
let us see
this sunset together

an event
which the first man
on earth had seen

and the last man will see

In the palms
of the night-magician
the sun is smashed
into fragments
and splashed
against darkness of the sky

again
on coming of the dawn
they are gathered into one

Be still
so that I can see
my face in thee

whispered the moon
to the restless sea

I have become turbulent
because of the beauty
in thee

replied the sea

Only when
we have nowhere to go
we reach our destination

from anywhere
the sky overhead
is always the centre of the sky

provided we look up
and forget
that there is some earth
underneath our feet

To walk inward
is a strange journey of knowing back

that acquires momentum
from the stillness of mind
and transforms
the inside of our being

like a bud
effortlessly flowering
to the last petal of its hidden fragrance

When my mind
drifts into
those rare moments of ecstasy

I become
not a flower
because a flower
has some mass for gravitation

I become
the name of a flower

In an evening like this
we were not here

in an evening like this
we shall not be here either

this evening
and on
let us be two nameless waves
and dance in the ocean of time

until we reach
the shore of eternity

Like the late afternoon sunshine
returning to the sun

like waves
falling back to the sea

like the wind trying to extricate itself
from a stormy night

like the great sound of thunder
melting in the simple silence of the sky

we are going to go
the same way

... and beyond

With each old leaf falling
the tree
gets to grow
a new leaf for the spring

why does the world
make so much fuss
over the nature's
simple law of
flowering and withering

Who is going fast
and who else is slow

hardly matters

all are going
and will have to go

When doctors failed
you consulted God

when God did not respond
you said

do not weep
that was all
the length of his stay here

What is going to happen
after death
is what has been happening
to us before our birth

life is
lightning's brief scribble over the sky
that is quickly
erased by the blue

Furious flood
sweeping away

tombstones
without a trace

to fulfil
the desire of the dead
to be nameless

Since so many of you
have left

the other side
looks
less lonely

a place
crowded with people
I would like
to re-live with

Whatever you think of me
is not what I am

what I know of myself
is not what I am

I am
is an outsider settled in me
in formless form

Rituals are done
to the dead
for satisfaction of the living

so that
the living could be treated
the same way
when they die

Inside the skin
we hold the skeleton
of some future time

deep
inside the skeleton

we hold
eternity for a while

When the time to go
will come

you need not have
to search for an exit

the whole universe
will be an exit

and you
will be unhoused into freedom

When the day dawns
time begins

when next day dawns
time begins

such moments
when nothing happens
time begins

only other things continue to end

Time is a river
without banks

yet
it does not
get flooded anywhere

its depth
depends
on how much we sink

What is that where
death comes from and life goes to

is it beyond all the soruces of light
or somewhere
beside blue path of the sky

may be
it is nowhere
or it is always here
by my wayside
ready to separate me from me

World has not become greater
with the teachings of the great

whose followers
have divided this earth
with their love and hate

how beautiful
it is for us to be
like those nameless leaves
on the tree that we see

know nothing of god
yet how godly they look to be

If I would have loved
a little more
than you had expected of me

or if you would have expected
a little less
just a little less than I had loved you

the heaven would not
have gone back to the sky

Black Eagle Books

www.blackeaglebooks.org
info@blackeaglebooks.org

Black Eagle Books, an independent publisher, was founded as a nonprofit organization in April, 2019. It is our mission to connect and engage the Indian diaspora and the world at large with the best of works of world literature published on a collaborative platform, with special emphasis on foregrounding Contemporary Classics and New Writing.

www.ingramcontent.com/pod-product-compliance
Lightning Source LLC
Chambersburg PA
CBHW020546080526
44583CB00013B/1027